CONGESTED
Yet My Heart Didn't Fail

Arianne E. McLean, MBA

Creative Touch Publishing LLC.

P.O. Box 7482
Warner Robins, GA 31095
ctpublishing14@gmail.com

Printed and bound in the United States of America

COPYRIGHT © 2022, Arianne E. McLean, MBA
ALL RIGHTS RESERVED

All rights reserved under international copyright law. No part of this book may be reproduced, stored in a retrieval system, or used in any manner without the express written permission of the author.

1. Spiritual. 2. Motivational. 3. Non-Fiction.

International Standard Book Number
978-0-578-94631-3

SATAN IS OVERCOME BY THE
BLOOD OF THE LAMB
AND THE WORD OF
OUR TESTIMONY.

Revelation 12:11 (KJV)

TABLE OF CONTENTS

Acknowledgements. 7

Foreword 9

My Stance 15

Chapter 1: Heart of the Matter 19

Chapter 2: Healing Heart 35

Chapter 3: Resilient Heart 53

Chapter 4: Praying Heart 63

Chapter 5: Heart Strengtheners 75

Chapter 6: Sing Divine Heart 83

Conclusion 93

ACKNOWLEDGEMENTS

First and foremost, to my Heavenly Father:
All glory and honor belongs to you, forever.

Eli J. Harper & Isaiah T. Harper:
My son-shines, my heartbeats; you are my everything. My love for you both is infinite. I am honored to be your mother; it is such a privilege. My prayer is that you will both always be blessed beyond measure.

Lord, I'm so grateful that you chose me.
Thank you, God!!!!!

Mr. James M. Brown Sr. & Retired Lieutenant Colonel Arizone H. Brown:
My Pops and my Mom. You are my paternal unit and I am so grateful for you both. There are no words I can say to truly express how much I love you both. Being your daughter is a divine blessing.

Thank you to my village. There are so many amazing, one of a kind, priceless individuals who make up my village. I love each of you. Without you, there would be no village. If you are part of my village, you know it. I love you and pray that God blesses each of you in a special way.

FOREWORD

"Train up a child in the way he should go and when he is old, he will not depart from it."

Proverb 22: 6 (KJV)

We count it all joy to be asked by our daughter Arianne Elizabeth McLean to write the foreword for, "Congested—Yet My Heart Didn't Fail."
I believe GOD has orchestrated the development of this book to happen now, in 2022, to be a tool of encouragement to many! Not just to women, but men too!

Arianne was born at Wright-Patterson Air Force Base in Dayton, Ohio. Before she was born, my prayer to God was for her to be a healthy baby. God answered my prayer as she was born healthy at 8 lbs.

She was beautiful, very happy, and very alert as a baby. She accomplished many of the milestones that measure human development earlier than normal. She was following with her eyes almost from day one and started walking at 10 months old. Arianne was very active and social as a toddler. She spent her toddler years in Woodbridge England, where I was reassigned by the United States Air Force. While there, we were informally adopted by a family in Wickham Market, a village in England. They became Arianne's God Parents.

While in England, Arianne picked up quite a few British mannerisms prior to our departure. We returned to the United States in 1992, our next assignment was Wright Patterson AFB. Upon our arrival, Arianne was enrolled at Our Lady of the Rosary Catholic School in Dayton, Ohio; where she attended first and second grade.

Arianne has always been spiritual. She was baptized at Wright Patterson Chapel in 1995 prior to us leaving Ohio. At the start of her third grade year we were reassigned to Seoul, South Korea at Yongsan Army Post. She attended third and fourth grades in South Korea, and fifth through eighth grades in Fairbanks, Alaska at

Eielson Air Force Base. Our final Air Force move was to Robins Air Force Base in Warner Robins, GA, where Arianne excelled in many of her class subjects and in basketball.

Arianne was also unique in that she decided to try out for the Warner Robins High School football team. However, she changed her mind because it was too much of a weather adjustment; having just come from Alaska.

Arianne completed high school with an athletic scholarship to Albany State University in Albany, GA where she competed in shot put during her freshman year. She then transferred to Fort Valley State University in Fort Valley, GA, where she graduated in 2009. In 2014 she went on to graduate from Wesleyan College in Macon, GA, where she received her master's degree.

Arianne was always a quick learner. She had the ability to adjust and re-adjusted to a number of challenges as she was growing up. Her father and I divorced in 1990, when she was four years old. The divorce had a really big impact on Arianne. She adjusted to the divorce and to moving around in the Air Force as best she could.

It was during graduate school when things really changed. As life's challenges became more difficult and adjusting to situations lead to her dark years as she explains in, this book.

In this personal testimony, Arianne shows that she is a survivor and that her belief in our Lord and Savior Jesus Christ was the center of her being while on the path to healing.

She shares her heart's secrets to give hope and encouragement to those who have been diagnosed with devastating illnesses and who have only been given a certain amount of time to live. Her desire is for you to know that you can live and that life can and will get better when you focus on God and the scriptures.

"Congested - Yet My Heart Didn't Fail" is stimulating—and a true example of what prayer can do.

When she called me and broke the news, with the diagnoses she received from her doctor, I replied, "That is what the doctors say—but you can strengthen your heart—everything is going to get better." I told her to remember that God is in control. What she had to do was believe and trust God to strengthen her heart.

This book is the result of all of Arianne's life experiences and pain. Now, she is using her story to help others out of their pain and to show that through faith and belief in GOD, you too can turn things around in your life.

MY STANCE

What was sent to destroy me only made me stronger!

I'm perfectly imperfect; a living testament to God's will and power. His love is truly unconditional. He has never forsaken me nor left me. His love is a shelter; a shield that keeps me from the enemy. He is protection from storms and a remedy that restores my heart and soul. I am committed to evolving and purposed for a higher calling.

Anointed by God, I am the woman for the job. This life...it chose me. If only the devil knew that I belonged to the Highest.

God is within her; she will not fall.

Psalm 46:5 (NIV)

REFLECTIONS

What traumatic situation have you faced? Reflect on how you made it through?

_____

_____

_____

In your quest to overcome and become, what credit do you give yourself for your evolution?

_____

_____

_____

What stance did you take as a result of the traumatic experience(s) you faced?

_____

_____

_____

CHAPTER ONE

HEART OF THE MATTER

2013 was a life altering year to say the least. I was in graduate school, and I was wild and free, reckless, young, and in love. Then I discovered I was pregnant. Unbeknownst to me at the time, that year would spark the genesis of me discovering who I truly am and what I have been divinely created to do.

I thought I knew everything I needed to know and thought I could control every situation in my life. That mindset had me on a slippery slope to darkness. It was a very unstable time in my life. I was deeply involved and committed to a man who I thought would be my husband. I gave him my all. I was down for and with him; ten toes down. No, man had ever gained accessed to my heart the way he did. However, I was the only one in the relationship who had developed strong feelings.

When I was five months pregnant with our son, I discovered he had gotten another woman pregnant. Oh, my goodness… I was livid! It rocked me to my core. Hurt was an understatement. I began to battle with questions like, why me? What did I do? How could you do this to me...to us? My heart was shattered into pieces. How does one even begin to fix or cure a broken heart while pregnant?

The birth of my first born was life changing. I had Eli seven weeks early. I woke up on the morning of April 5, 2014 struggling to breath. Putting on my clothes that morning was the hardest thing to do physically. I called my mom and told her I was struggling to breathe. She told me to go to the Emergency Room (ER) immediately. I drove myself to the ER, praying Lord, please let me make it.

Once I got to the ER I could barely speak. All I could say was I'm 32 weeks pregnant and I can't breathe. I can't recall anything else afterwards, it's all a blur.

I had to have an emergency cesarean section and woke up to the sound of Eli crying. I couldn't hold him right away, because I was admitted to the Intensive Care Unit (ICU) with Congested Heart Failure (CHF) and Eli was in the Newborn Intensive Care Unit (NICU). I was able to see him the next day, and I must say, I had never known what it is to love until they placed him on my chest skin to skin.

After the birth of Eli, I gained a new outlook on life, yet I struggled to make it to the next minute. I was in turmoil, both mentally and physically, as a result of heartbreak. That along with the stress of being a new mother, dealing with Congested heart failure, and trying to move forward in life, had me full of anxiety and spent.

I focused all of my energy on my son Eli. I knew that I had to be strong for him. I obtained my MBA that August in 2014. Truly that was only God. My mother and son witnessed me walk across the stage. It was one of the best days of my life.

Things never really got better between me and my son's father. There was a lot of deception and betrayal from him. There were also things that he was dealing with at the time that just wasn't the best look for him. However, I forgave him and held on to the idea of a family with him because of promises he made to do the right thing for both me and our son. He promised to be better as a man, and I truly loved and believed in him.

We reunited and shortly thereafter I discovered I was pregnant with our second child. We were so happy! Our little family was growing. When we found out we were having a boy he cried tears of joy. My pregnancy was high risk due to the onset of Congestive Heart Failure from my first pregnancy.

I thought things were going to get better between us. Then it happened again. It hit me like a ton of bricks. I couldn't believe I was pregnant by him for the second time and he was still cheating on me and had gotten another woman pregnant! There is no way to describe the feeling of disappointment and embarrassment.

Oh, my mind went to some dark places, and I had to keep reminding myself, "you're pregnant and you must think of your sons. Come back, don't go there." It was God and all His angels keeping me from a very dark place that would have kept me from the light of my son and my unborn child. I was pregnant and extremely depressed.

On August 6, 2015, my water broke unexpectedly. I had to stay in the hospital for two days, before having another cesarean section. I gave birth to my second son, Isaiah, who was also born at 32 weeks. He had to stay in the NICU as well. His birth helped to ease tensions between their father and me for a little while. Until it came to a point where dealing with their father and all that came with him became too overwhelming.

My children deserved a stable environment within their home. It wasn't easy but I made the decision to love my children and myself more.

Everything I knew as familiar, up to that point, became uncharted territory for me.

I grappled with the reality of being a single mother of two children, under the age of two. Heavy is the head that wears the crown! I was consumed with so many emotions and constantly thinking negative thoughts. Nothing was positive; even the sun looked grey. I was angry then depressed. Up then down. Emotionally, I experienced many highs and lows. I mean, I never knew I could be so angry and so depressed. I was literally sick, both mentally and physically.

Four months, after the birth of my second son, I began having difficulty breathing again. My body was retaining a lot of water. Walking from the bed to the kitchen or even to the mailbox was an extreme challenge, due to the shortness of breath I experienced. I notified my cardiologist and he scheduled a heart stress test. I knew I had experienced an onset of congested heart failure while carrying my first child. So having a second child wasn't an ideal situation at all.

I wasn't prepared for what the doctor had to say next. I remember as if it was yesterday, when the doctor walked in the room and asked if I had a relative who could come to the hospital. He told me once my relative arrived he would be able to read me the results of my stress test. My cousin, Dianna came to the hospital. Once she was in the room, the doctor then began to read the test results.

He informed me that my heart was only functioning at an Ejection Fraction (EF) of 13%. He looked me in the eyes and told me that I needed to make sure I get my affairs in order because I wouldn't be able to raise my children or do any of my day-to-day self-care or household tasks. I was a wreck. I just cried and cried.

Due to my heart being so weak, I couldn't be released from the hospital until I was fitted with an external defibrillator (a life vest).
Day and night I had to wear the life vest. I remember being afraid to take a shower because

I had to take it off. I was afraid to sleep, because I didn't know if I would wake up again. My anxieties were at an all-time high. I had the external life vest on for four weeks, then had a defibrillator implanted in my left shoulder. I didn't really know what to expect after the defibrillator was implanted. I was on edge and living with the fear that at any moment my heart could fail because it was so weak.

The thought that my defibrillator could shock me at any minute while in front of my sons or maybe even driving with my sons in the car replayed over and over in the forefront of my mind.

A month or so after the defibrillator was implanted, my mom, along with the boys and I, were headed to an event. We never made it to the event because my defibrillator started to chime and vibrate. There are no words to describe what I was thinking and feeling in that moment. I was so glad my mama was with us. She drove to my cardiologists' office and he determined that the defibrillator didn't shock me but was actually sending a warning signal that one of the leads connected to the defibrillator was over sensing, due to being placed incorrectly on my heart.

To prevent me from being shocked inappropriately, I had to have the lead removed and reattached correctly. I was scheduled for an emergency operation. I was relieved once the surgery was done, but I was still trying to cope and wrap my mind around having to live with a defibrillator implant. Though my sons were very young, I did my best to smile in front of them because I didn't want to show how I really felt on the inside. I even began to regret having children.

I was so broken inside and going through so much turmoil. All my thoughts were dark. I couldn't even recognize myself when looking in a mirror. I wasn't in a good space at all and I didn't know how I was going to make it. Mentally, spiritually, and physically I didn't...I was absent. I didn't know how to fix this type of damage or how to strengthen my heart. I felt so hoodwinked, but I knew deep down that I could not dwell in the pain of the heartbreak or allow the uncertainty regarding my health to stop me from being what I needed to be for my sons.

One day, I was sitting in my living room and the doorbell rang. It was my god-sister Brittney. In that very moment, she was truly God sent. She came in and said, "Sis I came to tell you today is the beginning of the rest of your life. I came to say you shall live and not die. I came by to encourage you to talk to our Heavenly Father, He is the only physician that can fix the impossible."

After she left, I put the boys down for their afternoon nap, went into my bedroom and closed the door. Alone in my room, on my knees with my hands stretch wide in the most VULNERABLE and HUMBLE state I've ever been in, I began to pray.
I cried out to God saying, "Help me, for so long I've tried doing things my way. Lord, I SURRENDER TO YOU. Forgive me Lord of all my

wrongdoings. Lord please clean me up and make me whole. Lord, God please fix my heart. I give you all of me. May YOUR WILL BE DONE IN MY LIFE. I ask that you dwell in me. Lord, I've seen you work in others and I want you to work within me."

At the time I was carrying the world on my shoulders and had so much turmoil within, but after praying, a peace came over me that transcended my ability to understand. I felt as if the weight of the world had been lifted off my shoulders.

Peace, I leave with you; my peace I give you. I do not give to you as the world gives. Do not let your heart be troubled and do not be afraid.

John 14:27 (NIV)

I have told you these things, so that in me you may have peace. In this world you will have many troubles but take heart! I have overcome the world.

John 16:33 (NIV)

Peace isn't the absence of trouble. It is the presence of God. God's supernatural peace surpasses natural comprehension.

The LORD is my shepherd, I lack nothing.
He makes me lie down in green pastures,
he leads me beside quiet waters, he refreshes
my soul. He guides me along the right paths
for his name's sake. Even though I walk
through the darkest valley, I will fear no evil,
for you are with me; your rod and your staff,
they comfort me. You prepare a table before
me in the presence of my enemies.
You anoint my head with oil; my up overflows.
Surely your goodness and love will follow
me all the days of my life, and I will dwell in
the house of the LORD, forever.

PSALM 23 (NIV)

REFLECTIONS

I was carrying the world on my shoulders and had so much turmoil within. Figuratively and literally, I was sick and in need of a healing that no one could resolve.

When you reflect on your life, what would you say has been the heart of matter?

_____
_____
_____
_____
_____
_____
_____

CHAPTER TWO

HEALING HEART

Healing: The process of making or becoming sound or healthy again (**Merriam Webster Dictionary**).

Everyone doesn't need healing from the same things or for the same reasons. Healing isn't a one size fits all process; it is not cookie cutter. My personal experience was living with a traumatic heart break, while battling congestive heart failure, and being a single mother of two young children, who were still in diapers.

This quickly became a situation of life or death that was so much bigger than me. I knew there was no way to overcome or conquer what was meant to destroy me, unless I surrendered my whole self to the omnipotent power that transcends all human capabilities. I knew I could only call on Jesus. He is the source of my life.

"Heal me, Lord, and I will be healed; save me and I will be saved, for you are the one I praise."

Jeremiah 17:14 (KJV)

"He changes times and seasons; he deposes kings and raises up others. He gives wisdom to the wise and knowledge to the discerning."

Daniel 2:21(NIV)

"My son, pay attention to what I say; turn your ear to my words. Do not let them out of your sight; keep them within your heart; for they are life to those who find them and health to one's whole body."

Proverbs 4:20-22 (NIV)

I kept hearing, "find your healing in the scriptures. Study the scriptures." Now, I've read scriptures before. All throughout my childhood my mother made sure I knew prayers, scriptures, and hymns. I also lead songs in the church choir, so I am no stranger to the Bible; but this time it was different. This time the Word captivated my mind in such an insightful way. Every word touched the core of my soul.

The Word began to breathe life into me. It began to heal me, cleanse me, strengthen me, and change me. The Word totally renewed my mind and heart.

For the word of God is alive and active. Sharper than any double-edged sword, it penetrates even to dividing soul and spirit, joints and marrow; it judges the thoughts and attitudes of the heart.

Hebrews 4:12 (NIV)

I will give you a new heart and put a new spirit in you; I will remove from you your heart of stone and give you a heart of flesh.

Ezekiel 36:26 (NIV)

In the beginning was the Word, and the Word was with God, and the Word was God.

John 1:1 (NIV)

The Word poured into my being; I was no longer in need. It healed me, gave me wisdom, clarification and sound understanding that was needed for each traumatic experience. The discomfort and bruises I suffered along the way no longer mattered.

We are all apart of God's plan and His plan will not be thwarted as we journey along with Him. Only God sees the big picture; He has the master plan.

And we know that in all things God works for the good of those who love him, who have been called according to his purpose.

Romans 8:28 (NIV)

For it is by grace you have been saved, through faith—and this is not from yourselves, it is the gift of God— not by works, so that no one can boast. For we are God's handiwork, created in Christ Jesus to do good works, which God prepared in advance for us to do.

Ephesians 2: 8-10 (NIV)

I found my reality; the very core of my existence in the Word of God.

Therefore, if anyone is in Christ, the new creation has come: The old has gone, the new is here!

2 Cor. 5:17 (NIV)

God is the fountain of life. I chose to live life on purpose. The things that hurt me in the past cannot control my future. I now understand what it means to walk in the light.

The light shines in the darkness, and the darkness has not overcome it.

John 1:5 (NIV)

Through him all things were made; without him nothing was made that has been made.

John 1:3 (NIV)

The word will make you examine yourself. It will sharpen you and make you walk upright. It's like, once you know better you endeavor to do better. For a long time I wasn't truly living; I was just going with the motions. I accepted things as they were and overlooked the red flags. This all played a major part in the traumatizing, life-changing events I experienced in life. Yet I'm so grateful for the lessons and blessings I have gained on this divine journey.

Pain and trouble are not the absent of God and doesn't come to harm us but to shape us into our authentic selves and propel us into purpose.

Consider it pure joy, my brothers and sisters, whenever you face trials of many kinds, because you know that the testing of your faith produces perseverance. Let perseverance finish its work so that you may be mature and complete, not lacking anything.

James 1:2-4 (NIV)

Our God is a God of abundance.

Praise the lord, O my soul all my innermost being, praise his holy name. Praise the Lord, O my soul, and forget not all His benefits, who forgives all your sins and heals all your diseases, who redeems your life from the pit and crowns you with love and compassion, who satisfies your desires with good things, so that your youth is renewed like the eagle's.

Psalm 103:1-5 (NIV)

The LORD is close to the brokenhearted and saves those who are crushed in spirit.

Psalm 34:18 (NIV)

I will always tell of God's goodness; I owe Him everything. I know for myself that He is the only physician that can fully heal a broken heart. He has never failed in his ability to heal the brokenhearted.

He heals the brokenhearted and binds up their wounds.

                                            Psalm 147:3 (NIV)

Studying and meditating on certain verses of scripture on a daily basis really resonated with me. It gave me clarity into the internal turmoil I'd experienced and provided me with the guidance I needed to heal. As my mind began to transform, my most recurring thoughts were forgiveness, self kindness, and not repeating cycles. These were at the forefront of my mind.

Dear Heart, Forgive for You

Forgiveness is a SUPERPOWER.
One of the most powerful tools on the path to healing is forgiveness. Forgiveness is important because it helps us move forward toward our future, rather than dwelling in the past. First you have to forgive yourself and know that every experience, whether good or bad, was and is working for your benefit.

And we know that in all things God works for the good of those who love him, who have been called according to his purpose.

Romans 8:28 (NIV)

Secondly, you have to forgive the person(s) who broke your heart and caused damage to your physical/mental wellbeing. This is easier said than done. However, you need to understand that letting go of resentment and thoughts of revenge will set you free. A heart that isn't willing to forgive and let go will not heal.

Forgiveness doesn't mean forgetting or excusing the harm done to you. It doesn't mean we have to make up with the person who caused the harm. Forgiveness gives you permission to be at peace and to move on with life. I've come to learn from experience, that people don't really understand how their actions can negatively affect others.

There are also a lot of health benefits that come with forgivingness, such as improved mental health, less anxiety, less stress, improved heart health and improved self-esteem.

Forgiveness affects every area of our lives, including our relationships and our spiritual health. It's your time! Forgive and let go so you can heal. Dear heart, heal.

Dear Heart, Be Kind to Yourself In Your Process of Healing.

Self-love is a MUST! We should practice self-love daily. You can start by being kind, patient, gentle, and compassionate to yourself; just as you would someone else that you care about. I believe self-love is appreciation for oneself that grows from our actions that support our physical, mental, and spiritual growth.

When holding ourselves in high esteem we are more likely to align with those things that nurture our wellbeing and better serve us. These things may present themselves in the form of eating healthier, getting plenty of rest, exercising, positive self-talk, and creating healthy self-care habits. In due time, your dear heart will heal.

It is imperative to understand that, with time, all wounds do heal. Be kind to yourself and take the time to love on you. Learning to love ourselves is important when it comes to healing a broken heart because it helps strengthen our hearts and creates an inward focus of authentic self-love.

Dear Heart Don't Repeat Cycles

Learn from your mistakes and grow.
Doing the same thing repeatedly will guarantee you the same results. That goes for every area of your life. If the familiar is uncomfortable or draining, make a change.

In the midst of learning and growing, take the time to reflect. Think about what you went through and remember how you felt while going through it. For some, the change might be walking away from a negative relationship or situation, while not creating excuses to stay, but recognizing opportunities to move forward.

Remember, there is always a blessing in the middle of the mess. If you miss the lessons, know that the devil is always taking notes and waiting to use the same cycles against you.

Trust me; the devil does not want you to learn from your mistakes. He wants to keep you caught up in cycles. We are told to, **"put off your old self, which belongs to your former manner of life and is corrupt through deceitful desires, and to be renewed in the spirit of your minds, and to put on the new self, created after the likeness of God in true righteousness and holiness" (Ephesians 4:22-24).**

Do not conform to the pattern of this world, but be transformed by the renewing of your mind. Then you will be able to test and approve what God's will is—his good, pleasing and perfect will.

Romans 12:2 (ESV)

My Prayer for Healing:

Heavenly Father, Gracious God, I call on you right now and ask that you heal my heart, by your grace. May my heart be healed. It is through your power that I was created. I'm more than grateful for every breath I take each morning I wake and each moment of every hour. I will forever show my love and appreciation for you and your gift of infinite grace by keeping your commandments and joyfully walking in the newness of life. Amen.

REFLECTIONS

There is power in the name of Jesus to break every cycle. Healing isn't a one size fits all process. However, healing is necessary. I've come to learn that God's Word is healing and health to all our flesh. The very core of our existence and healing is found in God's living Word.

"Submit yourselves to God. Come near to God and he will come near to you."

James 4:7-8 (NIV)

Are you willing to let go of your old habits and thought patterns?

_____

_____

_____

_____

Are you committed to healing?

_____

_____

_____

_____

If you could encourage someone on their healing journey what would you say to them?

_____

_____

_____

_____

_____

CHAPTER THREE

RESILIENT HEART

The dictionary defines the resilient as the ability to withstand or recover after experiencing challenges, adversity, stress, pain or setbacks **(Merriam Webster Dictionary).**

Resilience empowers us to accept, adapt, and move forward in life.

"Though the righteous fall seven times, THEY RISE AGAIN, but the wicked stumble when calamity strikes."
Proverbs 24:16 (NIV)

My constant prayer is that my heart becomes stronger and healthier with each new day God grants me to live. As a single mother, I am grateful to have the ability to raise my sons and work, while at the same time, living with congestive heart failure.

The doctors told me I wouldn't be able to, BUT ،GOD! There aren't words that can truly describe how grateful I am that God is who he is.

He has given us a "way in the wilderness and streams in the wasteland"

Isaiah 43:19 (NIV)

I am amazed at what God has done, is doing, and is going to do for my sons and I. I continuously find myself in awe because the Lord continues to keep me and make a way for my life. I put all my trust in him. Trusting God signifies that you know, by faith, that God loves you and that he will always do what is right concerning you.

I am the LORD, and there is no other; apart from me there is no God. I will strengthen you.

Isaiah 45:5 (NIV)

"Fear not, for I am with you; be not dismayed, for I am your God. I will strengthen you, yes, I will help you, I will uphold you with my righteous right hand."

Isaiah 41:10 (NKJV)

"Resist him, standing firm in the faith, because you know that the family of believers throughout the world is undergoing the same kind of sufferings."

1 Peter 5:9 (NIV)

"For I know the plans I have for you," declares the LORD, "plans to prosper you and not to harm you, plans to give you hope and a future."

Jeremiah 29:11(NIV)

"The LORD himself goes before you and will be with you; he will never leave you nor forsake you. Do not be afraid; do not be discouraged."

Deuteronomy 31:8 (NIV)

God turned my pain into gain. His Word became my profit. I found God and got to know my heavenly father for myself. As a result, I became anchored in his living Word. He transformed my life and gave me divine strength to stand and be resilient.

May the favor of the Lord our God rest upon us; establish the work of our hands for us yes, establish the work of our hands.

> Psalms 90:17 (NIV)

Jesus is Lord over my spirit, my soul, and my body.

> Philippians 2:9-11 (NIV)

The love of God has been shed abroad in my heart by the Holy Spirit and his love abides in me richly. I keep myself in the kingdom of light, in love, in the word, and the wicked one touches me not.

> Romans 5:5; 1 John 4:16; John 5:18 (NIV)

I fear not for God has given me a spirit of power, of love, and of a sound mind. God is on my side.

> 2 Timothy 1:7; Romans 8:31 (NIV)

My Prayer for Resilience:

Lord God, thank you for making my heart resilient. Thank you Heavenly Father for giving me the grit to be the mother I need to be for Eli and Isaiah. Lord, I ask that you always surround us with your divine presence.

Finally, brother and sisters, whatever is true, whatever is noble, whatever is right, whatever is pure, whatever is lovely, whatever is admirable if anything is excellent or praiseworthy think about such things. Whatever you have learned or received or heard from me, or seen in me, put into practice, and the God of peace will be with you.

Amen

Philippians 4:8-9 (NIV)

REFLECTIONS

Change is constant. It is the most consistent thing in life. Learning to cope with the expected and unexpected changes in life is key. Your superpower is your ability to get up and keep going. You will achieve your goals in-spite of life's circumstances.

"For the Spirit God gave us does not make us timid, but gives us power, love and self-discipline."

2 Timothy 1:7 (NIV)

God is on our side. He has bestowed grace and mercy upon each of us. Here are some qualities that will help you build resiliency:

- A positive attitude
- Being optimistic
- Controlling your emotions
- Having a growth mindset

Do you have a resilient heart? Explain.

_____

_____

_____

_____

_____

Describe times when you have shown resiliency.

_____

_____

_____

_____

_____

CHAPTER FOUR

PRAYING HEART

Prayer is essential. We must to learn to **worry less and pray more** (Philippians 4:6).

Prayer is not to be done in a religious form; with no power. It is to be effective, accurate, and bring results because **God watches over His Word to perform it** (Jeremiah 1:12).

Prayer is the living Word in our mouths. Our mouths must speak forth faith, because **faith is what pleases God** (Hebrews 11:6).

Prayer is our direct connection to our Heavenly Father. It is our means of tapping into his power. We hold God's Word up to him in prayer, and our Father sees himself in his Word.

As you pray in line with God's Word, he joyfully hears you. You are his child; living and walking in the Truth (3 John 4).

Believe you receive when you pray. Confess the Word and hold fast to your confession of faith in God's Word. Allow your spirit to pray by the Holy Spirit and praise God for the victory before you see the manifestation. **Walk by faith and not by sight (2 Corinthians. 5:7).**

God moves as we pray in faith. **His eyes run to and fro throughout the whole earth to show himself strong on behalf of those whose hearts are blameless toward Him (2 Chronicles 16:9).**

We are his children; we are his righteousness in Christ Jesus (Ephesians 1:5; 2 Corinthians 5:21).

God tells us to, **"Come boldly to the throne of grace to obtain mercy and find grace to help in our time of need" (Hebrew 4:16).** We have appropriate and well-timed help available to us! PRAISE THE LORD!!!!

Be strong in the lord and in his mighty powers. Put on the full armor of God so that you can take your stand against the devil's schemes. For our struggle is not against flesh and blood, but against the rulers, against the authorities, against the powers of this dark world and

against the spiritual forces of evil in the heavenly realms. Therefore, put on the full armor of God, so that when the day of evil comes, you may be able to stand your ground and after you have done everything to stand. Stand firm then, with the belt of truth buckled around your waist, with the breastplate or righteousness in place, and with your feet fitted with the readiness that comes from the gospel of peace. In addition to all this, take up the shield of faith, with which you can extinguish all the flaming arrows of the evil one. Take the helmet of salvation and the sword of the spirit, which is the word of God. And pray in the spirit on all occasions with all kinds of prayers and requests. With this in mind, be alert and always keep on praying for all the saints.

Ephesians 6:10-18 (NIV)

The issues of life all begin within the heart.

"Man looks on the outward appearance, but the Lord looks in the heart"

1 Samuel 16:7 (NIV)

The heart is important to Jesus. What we are deep within is what he cares about most. Jesus came into the world to purify our hearts.

"Search me, O God, and know my heart; test me and know my anxious thoughts."

Psalm 139:23 (NIV)

"For the eyes of the lord are on the righteous and his ears are attentive to their prayer."

1 Peter 3:12 (NIV)

"He desires that we know how to pray for the prayer of the upright is his delight."

Proverbs 15:8 (NIV)

"Whatever you ask in my name, this I will do, that the Father may be glorified in the Son."

John 14:13 (NIV)

My Prayer for Praying:

Dear Holy Spirit, teach me how to pray. Help me to grow in my prayer life. I want to be bold and confident in the things of God. I welcome you in my entire life. Move boldly in my life. Come Holy Spirit, and fill me with your love and your kindness. Guide me into all truth according to John 6:13. Amen.

REFLECTIONS

Prayer is our direct line of communication with our Heavenly Father. God wants us to seek Him in prayer with our whole hearts.

Here are some prayer points that will help improve your prayer life.

God wants to dwell in your heart forever. Have you invited Him into your heart?

_____

_____

_____

_____

_____

Meditate on the fact that God dwells in your heart; in all circumstances. Now, ask God to dwell in all aspects of your life.

Prayer Results:

_____
_____
_____
_____
_____

You are worthy of his love. Why not you? Meditate on the fact that God has a purpose for your life. Now, ask God to give you understanding to fulfill His purpose for your life.

Prayer Results:

_____
_____
_____
_____
_____

Heavenly Father, I need your love every minute, every hour, and every day. I can't make it without you. Your presence and love are so divine.

Meditate on God's endless and unconditional love towards you. Now, ask God to help you love others the way He loves you.

Prayer Results:

_____

_____

_____

_____

_____

There is none greater than you, God. Nothing or no one can compare to you. My worship and praise belong to you.

Meditate on the amazing goodness of God. Now, tell him how grateful you are that he knows your name.

Prayer Results:

_____

_____

_____

_____

_____

CHAPTER FIVE

HEART STRENGTHENERS

GOD IS SAYING TO YOU:

You will rise my child and be healed. Better days are coming. Blessings upon blessing are coming your way!

Life experiences, situations, and needing ways to cope so that I am able go forth, has been the driving force behind why I seek to connect with God more and more. I want to spend all my time with him and then some. I am always seeking out ways to be in his presence.

Over time, daily devotionals became that one appointment I couldn't and wouldn't miss or reschedule. I must have that one-on-one time with God every day; even if it's only for 5 minutes. I need to be in his presence.

Daily devotion helps us develop a deeper understanding of the God and his Word. It helps us grow spiritually, and makes us stronger in areas where we may be weak. It also helps give us a sense of peace in our lives.

My day is better when I talk to God first. Learn to meditate on a bible verse, pray, and command your day. I keep a bible verse journal to study verses that really resonate with me.

I'm sharing this with you because I pray that all is well with your soul and that your heart is strengthened as well.

GOD IS SAYING TO YOU:

YOU ARE CHOSEN.
But you are a chosen people, a royal priesthood, a holy nation, a people belonging to God, that you may declare the praise of him who called you out of darkness into his wonderful light.

1 Peter 2:9 (NIV)

YOU ARE LOVED.
But God demonstrates his own love for us in this; while we were still sinners, Christ died for us.

Romans 5:8 (NIV)

YOU ARE FAVORED.
For surely, O lord, you bless the righteous you surround them with your favor as with a shield.

Psalm 5:12 (NIV)

YOU ARE HEALED.
He himself bore our sins in his body on the tree, so that we might die to sins and live for righteousness; by his wounds you have been healed.

1 Peter 2:24 (NIV)

YOU ARE REDEEMED.
In him we have redemption through his blood, the forgiveness of sins, in accordance with the riches of God's grace.

Ephesians 1:7 (NIV)

YOU ARE BLESSED.
Blessed is he whose help is the God of Jacob, whose hope is in the lord his God.

Psalm 146:5 (NIV)

YOU HAVE AN AMAZING DESTINY.

For I know the plans I have for you, declares the lord, plans to prosper you and not harm you plans to give you hope and a future.

Jeremiah 29:11 (NIV)

GOD IS SAYING TO YOU:

I know what you need; trust that I will provide for you (Luke 12: 22-34).

GOD IS MY PEACE.
GOD IS MY COMFORT.
GOD IS MY STRENGTH.
GOD IS MY JOY.

But you, Beloved, build yourselves up in your most holy faith; praying in the Holy Spirit.

Jude 20 (NIV)

Blessed is the one who perseveres under trial because, having stood the test, that person will receive the crown of life that the Lord has promised to those who love him.

James 1:12 (KJV)

However, as it is written: "What no eye has seen, what no ear has heard, and what no human mind has conceived" the things God has prepared for those who love him."

1 Corinthians 2:9 (NIV)

So is my word that goes out from my mouth. It will not return to me empty but will accomplish what I desire and achieve the purpose for which I sent it.

Isaiah 55:11 (NIV)

THE LORD'S PRAYER

"Our Father in heaven,
hallowed be your name,
your kingdom come,
your will be done,
on earth as it is in heaven.
Give us today our daily bread.
And forgive us our debts,
as we also have forgiven our debtors.
And lead us not into temptation,
but deliver us from the evil one.
For thine is the kingdom,
And the power,
and the glory, forever.
Amen

Matthew 6:9-13 (NIV)

CHAPTER SIX

SING DIVINE HEART

A Hymn of Praise to Our God

I have waited patiently for the Lord: He turned to me and heard my cry. He lifted me out of the slimy pit, out of the mud and mire; He set my feet on a rock and gave me a firm place to stand. He put a new song in my mouth.

Psalm 40:1-3 (NIV)

I'm so grateful I can barely contain my joy! There's a fire that burns deep within me that has ignited my heart and soul to sing only for the Lord. I will always sing praises to the Highest. He is my Heavenly Father. All of my strength comes from him. I owe him everything and I will always sing for him.

I will praise you, o Lord, with all my heart. I will tell of your wonders. I will be glad and rejoice in you; I will sing praise to your name, o Most High.

Psalm 9:1-2 (NIV)

Praise the Lord.

Praise the Lord, o my soul. I will praise the Lord all my life; I will sing praise to my God as long as I live.

Psalm 146:1-2 (NIV)

Speaking to one another with psalms, hymns, and songs from the Spirit. Sing and make music from your heart to the Lord, always giving thanks to God the Father for everything, in the name of our Lord Jesus Christ.

Ephesians 5:19-20 (NIV)

My heart is now stronger than ever because of God's love. It is filled with joy! An overwhelming flow of God's love causes my heart to sing.

Poems & Songs from My Heart

The following is a collection of poems and songs that have come from my heart.

My Safe Haven

The safest place
Is in the will of God
Keep me Lord
Use me in your will
Holy Spirit
Teach me your ways
Guide me
Holy Spirit
Lead me
For I am your child
Holy Spirit
I trust in you.

The Word Is Essential

Something happens when I read the Holy Word
I know I can get through when I read
My pops told me to read your Living Word
Pops told me doors will open for me that
No man can close
Something happens when I read the Holy Word

Your Spirit

Your Spirit lives within me
Hallelujah I am not alone
He's my comfort
I am not alone
Hallelujah

I surrender my all to you Lord
I surrender my life to you Lord
Everything I give to you Lord
All or nothing

King Jesus, I give you all of me
King Jesus my Savior forever
I give you all of me

Dwell in my heart
Dwell in my children
Dwell in my business
Dwell in everything attached to me
With God's power at work within me,
I will be free and live my life on purpose

Dwell in my heart
Dwell in my children
Dwell in my business
Dwell in everything attached to me

Can't Stop, Won't Stop

Not a devil or demon in hell or walking upright
can slow or stop what my Heavenly Father has
for me and mine.

No eye has seen, nor ear heard
No mind has imagined what God has prepared
for me.

For the rest of my life, I'll praise his name.
I'll never be able to repay him, for all that He's
done and for all that he will do.

Even if I had ten thousand tongues, I wouldn't be
able to praise him enough.

Thank you, Lord, for keeping me and my sons;
for including us in your plans.

Bless you!!!
I'm forever grateful for you!!!
I love you!!!
What's for me is for me!!!

Your Divine Plan

Lord, God I may not understand
what it is you're doing.
No matter what it is, I trust you!
You have the master plan my Lord.
I pray that you will always include my sons and I
in your divine plan.

Lord I pray and speak life over all.
Lord, God I pray for anyone and everyone who
is connected to me and
who will become connected to me and
mine.

We will always be blessed, In Jesus name,
upon generations and generations
Amen, Amen
Amen, Amen
In your Holy Name,
Amen

He Makes Everything Alright

Something happens

when I call on the name of

Jesus!!!

You are my Lord

Jesus!!!

You keep your strong hand on me

Jesus!!!!

At the mention of his name demons tremble

Jesus!!!!

All I have to do is call on

Jesus!!!!!

He will make it alright

My Heart Belongs to You Lord

Forever is a long time
That's how long I'll love you
Forever
Bright morning star
The head of my life
Oh Lord
You are my anchor
My heart fixer
Forever is a long time
That's how long I'll love you
Forever is a long time
That's how long I'll love you

Lord, you brought me out
Lord I'll never forget

I won't forget
Never could I forget
My heart belongs to you
my Lord

CONCLUSION

OF THE

MATTER

This book is my personal testimony detailing how God's love and Word gave me peace that surpassed my understanding, healed my brokenness, and positively transformed my entire existence.

God has decongested my life, strengthened my weakened heart, and healed my brokenness in such a special way that only he could.

I now live my life on purpose every day.
One step of faith will change your life forever.

I pray that every person who reads this testimony will accept Jesus Christ as your personal Lord and Savior, today. I may not know your name or your circumstances, but God told me to write this book for you.

I know from experience, that when you accept Jesus Christ into your life, you will come closer to what God has for you.

I encourage you, with a sense of urgency, to get into God's Word and begin developing your personal relationship with OUR HEAVENLY FATHER, and I pray that you will adhere to His Living Word.

Always remember, GOD IS ON YOUR SIDE AND WORKING ON YOUR BEHALF.

In Jesus Name,

Amen

"IT IS BY GRACE YOU HAVE BEEN SAVED, THROUGH FAITH AND THIS IS NOT FROM YOURSELVES, IT IS THE GIFT OF GOD."

Ephesians 2:8 (NIV)

DON'T SQUANDER THIS GIFT!

"LORD, YOU ESTABLISH PEACE FOR US; FOR ALL THAT WE HAVE ACCOMPLISHED YOU HAVE DONE FOR US."

Isaiah 26:12 (NIV)

A personal testimony is a practical, transparent, and encouraging account of one's own extraordinary experience and relationship with the Heavenly Father. In sharing my account, you have learned that:

- GOD GUIDES US
- GOD PROTECTS US
- GOD HEALS US

"FOR GOD WORKS ALL THINGS TOGETHER FOR GOOD TO THOSE WHO LOVE HIM AND ARE CALLED ACCORDING TO HIS PURPOSE."

Romans 8:28 (NIV)

Moment of Reflection

I went from being reckless, wild, and free to being a single mother of two, and a heart warrior battling congestive heart failure. I'll never forget the day my doctor told me my heart was only functioning at 13%. He looked me in my eyes, told me I wouldn't be able to raise my children, or perform any of my day-to-day self-care or household tasks.

Broken was an understatement, I was more than depressed. The sun was grey every day.
I didn't recognize myself anymore. I was carrying the weight of the world on my shoulders and had so much turmoil within. Figuratively and literally, I was sick and in need of a healing that no one could remedy; but God. I surrendered my all to God's will and asked Him to forgive me of all my transgressions. He cleaned me up, changed my mindset, placed my feet on solid ground, and gave me the strength to live life on purpose.

REFLECTIONS

What's the heart of the matter in your life?

_____

_____

_____

_____

Have you tried to fix the heart of the matter yourself?

_____

_____

_____

_____

If so, did you succeed at remedying the heart of the matter?

_____

_____

_____

_____

Always remember, God wants you to give Him all your burdens and the heart of the matter in your life. He loves you and is working on your behalf!